Farmyard Friends

PIGS

Maddie Gibbs

PowerKiDS press.
New York

Published in 2015 by The Rosen Publishing Group, Inc.
29 East 21st Street, New York, NY 10010

First Edition

Editor: Caitie McAneney
Book Design: Katelyn Heinle

Photo Credits: Cover, pp. 1, 10, 24 (piglets) talseN/Shutterstock.com; p. 5 goory/Shutterstock.com; p. 6 Yu Lan/Shutterstock.com; p. 9 BMJ/Shutterstock.com; pp. 13, 24 (snout) Igor Stramyk/Shutterstock.com; p. 14 ER_09/Shutterstock.com; pp. 17, 22 bikeriderlondon/Shutterstock.com; p. 18 Fuse/Getty Images; pp. 21, 24 (wild boars) Eduard Kyslynskyy/Shutterstock.com.

Library of Congress Cataloging-in-Publication Data

Gibbs, Maddie, author.
Pigs / Maddie Gibbs.
pages cm. — (Farmyard friends)
Includes index.
ISBN 978-1-4994-0170-7 (pbk.)
ISBN 978-1-4994-0171-4 (6 pack)
ISBN 978-1-4994-0168-4 (library binding)
1. Swine—Juvenile literature. 2. Domestic animals—Juvenile literature. [1. Pigs.] I. Title.
SF395.5.G55 2015
636.4—dc23

2014025290

Manufactured in the United States of America

CPSIA Compliance Information: Batch #CW15PK: For Further Information contact Rosen Publishing, New York, New York at 1-800-237-9932

CONTENTS

Pigs are smart animals.

Some pigs live on big farms.
Some pigs live on small farms.

Female pigs are called sows.
Males are called boars.

Baby pigs are called **piglets**.
They grow fast!

A pig's nose is called a **snout**. Pigs have a great sense of smell.

Pigs roll in the mud to cool off.

People raise pigs for their meat. Some people keep them as pets.

Pigs can be different colors.
Duroc pigs are red.

People raised the first farm pigs from **wild boars**. These animals live in forests.

Pigs are friendly. Pet one the next time you visit a farm!

WORDS TO KNOW

piglets

snout

wild boars

INDEX

WEBSITES

Due to the changing nature of Internet links, PowerKids Press has developed an online list of websites related to the subject of this book. This site is updated regularly. Please use this link to access the list: www.powerkidslinks.com/fmyd/pig